To Our Parents

TEACH ME ABOUT PRAYER
© 1990 by Linda Sattgast & Jan Elkins
Published by Multnomah Press
Portland, Oregon 97266

Printed in Hong Kong

Library of Congress Cataloging-in-Publication Data

Sattgast, L. J., 1953-
    Teach me about prayer / by L.J. Sattgast and Jan Elkins ; illustrated by Russ Flint.
      p.   cm.
    Includes selected Bible verses
    Summary: A simple introduction to the reasons and occasions for prayer.
    ISBN 0-88070-382-2
    1. Prayer—Christianity—Juvenile literature. [1. Prayer.] I. Elkins, Jan.
II. Flint, Russ, ill. III. Bible. English. Selections. 1990. IV. Title
BV212.S27   1990
248.3'.2—dc20
                                      90-33887
                                      CIP
                                      AC

90 91 92 93 94 95 96 97 98 99 - 9 8 7 6 5 4 3 2 1

Teach me about
PRAYER

By L.J. Sattgast & Jan Elkins
Illustrations by Russ Flint

MULTNOMAH
Portland, Oregon 97266

I talk to people every day—
my mother and my father,
my sister and my brother.
I even talk to my dog.
And there's someone else
I talk to.

I talk to God every day.

When I get up I say,

"Good morning, God!"

When I go to bed I say,

"Good night, God!"

Talking to God is called prayer.

Pray continually (1 Thessalonians 5:17).

Sometimes I pray when I'm running and playing.
I can talk to God anytime I want, and he always listens.

...the LORD will hear when I call to him (Psalm 4:3).

I pray with my family
before I eat. We say,
"Thank you, God,
for this good food!"

...God created [food] to be received with thanksgiving by those who believe... (1 Timothy 4:3).

I pray for other people.
When someone is sick, I say,
"Dear God, please help my
friend to get well."

...pray for each other so that you may be healed (James 5:16).

Sometimes I am afraid.
Then I remember that God
is always with me.
"Dear God, I trust you!
Help me not to be afraid!"

When I am afraid, I will trust in you (Psalm 56:3).

God likes to hear
about how I feel.
When I'm happy,
I tell him so,
and he is happy, too.

Sing to God...and rejoice before him (Psalm 68:4).

When I am sad,

I tell God about it.

He knows how I feel

because he's been sad, too.

...he knows what it is like when we suffer and are tempted, and he is wonderfully able to help us (Hebrews 2:18, TLB).

Sometimes I do things
that are not kind.
I tell God I'm sorry.
"Dear God, I was wrong.
Please forgive me!"
And he always does.

If we confess our sins, he is faithful and just and will forgive us our sins. . . (1 John 1:9).

When someone else hurts me,
I forgive them just like God
forgives me.

Forgive us our sins, just as we have forgiven those who have sinned against us (Matthew 6:12, TLB).

Most of all, I like to praise God.

Sometimes I sing,

and sometimes I talk out loud,

and sometimes I just whisper,

"Dear God, you're so wonderful,

and I love you!"

I will praise the LORD all my life; I will sing praise to my God as long as I live (Psalm 146:2).

Helpful hints for parents about
PRAYER

YOUR CHILD'S READINESS TO PRAY
- Pray for your child from conception on. (Or even before!)
- Start training as soon as your child is able to talk.
- Each child is unique. Some will respond openly and even eagerly. Others will respond at a slower pace. Be consistent and don't give up. You will never regret your efforts!

PROCEDURES IN TEACHING PRAYER
- Set aside a special time to pray each day. Bedtime seems to work well for many parents.
- Decide how you will address God—"Dear God," "Jesus," "Father," etc.
- Begin by teaching your child to repeat a simple phrase. Add more phrases as your child grows.
- When you think your child is ready to pray on her own, ask leading questions like, "What would you like to thank God for?" etc.
- Throughout the day, pray with your child for the little things that concern him. Help him identify and pray about hurt feelings.
- Pray for your child when she is sick or hurt, and then teach her to pray for you when you are sick or upset.
- Give your child a chance to give thanks before meals.
- Be specific when you pray so that your child can see specific answers and be encouraged to pray more.

PRAYER ACTIVITIES
- Collect pictures of family, friends, and missionaries. Let your child pick out someone to pray for each day.
- Purchase or make a booklet with blank pages. At the top of the page write: "Dear God, thank you for:" or "Dear God, help me to:" Let him draw a picture and tell you what it means. Briefly write down his explanation. You and your child will enjoy going back over the prayers.

RESISTANCE TO PRAYER
- If your child is not accustomed to praying, she may need assistance with how to pray or what to pray about.
- Your child may avoid praying because he is too "wound up" from the day's activities. Take a few minutes to quiet him down with a lullaby or back rub. If he still resists praying, ask him to listen quietly while you pray.
- If your child is angry or disobedient, there can be a natural yet spiritual resistance to prayer.
- Never criticize your child's prayers or punish him for refusing to pray.

EXAMPLES OF PRAYER
- Waking up with a bad attitude —"Dear God, I didn't wake up happy. Help me to wake up happy."
- Sibling rivalry —"Dear God, I forgive my sister/brother. You always forgive and love me."
- Lack of obedience —"Dear God, I disobeyed. Change my heart. Help me to obey quickly."
- Grumbling, pouting, and temper tantrums —"Dear God, I was feeling sorry for myself. I want to be thankful. Thank you for..."

ADDITIONAL SUGGESTIONS
- A child may believe God doesn't love her when she is naughty. Remind her that God's love never changes!
- Forgiveness will become a large part of your child's prayer life. Teach your child that we forgive because we *choose* to, not because we feel like it.
- Make up a "blessing" for your child and repeat it every night before he or she goes to bed. Pick out the qualities you want God to develop in your child. Example: "May you grow to be a man (woman) of God, full of (faith, courage, grace, etc.). Even if your child doesn't understand the words, he will know he is being blessed, and eventually will ask you what the words mean.
- Prayer is a normal, everyday occurrence. Let your child see you praying openly and spontaneously. Your example is the best teacher.